MW01231213

Air Fryer Snack And Dessert Cookbook For Beginners

Healthy And Sweets Air Fryer Recipes for Beginners

SHEILA COOK

Air Fryer Snack And Dessert Cookbook For Beginners

Table Of Contents

DESCRIPTION

The history of Air fryers dates back to a few years ago; exactly during the third quarter of the year 2010 and it was a completely revolutionary invention that was invented by Philips Electronics Company. Philips introduced the Air Fryer to the world and changed the conception of the culinary world all at once.

The Air Fryer is used as a substitute for your oven, stovetop, and deep fryer. It comes with various handy parts and other tools that you can buy to use your Air Fryer for different cooking styles, which include the following:

• Grilling. It provides the same heat to grill food ingredients without the need to flip them continuously. The hot air goes around the fryer, giving heating on all sides. The recipes include directions of how many times you ought to shake the pan during the cooking process.

To make the process of grilling faster, you can use a grill pan or a grill layer. They will soak the excess fat from the meat that you are cooking to give you delicious and healthy meals.

- Baking. The Air Fryer usually comes with a baking pan (or you can buy or use your ownto make treats that are typically done using an oven. You can bake goodies, such as cakes, bread, cupcakes, muffins, and brownies in your Air Fryer.
- Roasting. It roasts food ingredients, which include vegetables and meat, faster than when you do it in the oven.
- Frying is its primary purpose – to cook fried foods with little or no oil.

You can cook most food items in an Air Fryer. There are some foods that you should refrain from cooking in the fryer because they will taste better when cooked in the traditional ways — they include fried foods with batter and steamed veggies, such as beans and carrots.

Despite this, you will never run out of ingredients to cook using your Air Fryer – from veggies to seafood, chicken, egg, turkey, and a lot more. The most common component that is prepared using this appliance is potatoes.

The Air Fryer also comes with a separator, and this allows you to cook multiple dishes at the same time. You need to choose recipes that can be prepared at the same temperature setting.

This book covers the following topics:

- Breakfast
- Mains
- Sides
- Seafood
- Poultry
- Meat
- Vegetables
- Snacks
- Desserts and more!!!

INTRODUCTION

There are many kinds of foods that you can cook using an air fryer, but there are also certain types that are not suited for it. Avoid cooking ingredients, which can be steamed, like beans and carrots. You also cannot fry foods covered in heavy batter in this appliance.

Aside from the above mentioned, you can cook most kinds of ingredients using an air fryer. You can use it to cook foods covered in light flour or breadcrumbs. You can cook a variety of vegetables in the appliance, such as cauliflower, asparagus, zucchini, kale, peppers, and corn on the cob. You can also use it to cook frozen foods and home prepared meals by following a different set of instructions for these purposes.

An air fryer also comes with another useful feature - the separator. It allows you to cook multiple dishes at a time. Use the separator to divide ingredients in the pan or basket. You have to make sure that all ingredients have the same temperature setting so that everything will cook evenly at the same time.

The Benefits of Air fryer

It is important to note that air fried foods are still fried. Unless you've decided to eliminate the use of oils in cooking, you must still be cautious about the food you eat. Despite that, it clearly presents a better and healthier option than deep-frying. It helps you avoid unnecessary fats and oils, which makes it an ideal companion when you intend to lose weight. It offers a lot more benefits, which include the following:

- It is convenient and easy to use, plus, it's easy to clean.
- It doesn't give off unwanted smells when cooking.
- You can use it to prepare a variety of meals.
- It can withstand heavy cooking.

- It is durable and made of metal and high-grade plastic.
- Cooking using this appliance is not as messy as frying in a traditional way. You don't have to worry about greasy spills and stains in the kitchen.

CHAPTER 1

SNACKS

1. Peppers and Cheese Dip

Preparation Time: 25 minutes Servings: 6

INGREDIENTS:

- 2 bacon slices, cooked and crumbled
- 4 oz. parmesan; grated
- 4 oz. mozzarella; grated
- 8 oz. cream cheese, soft
- 2 roasted red peppers; chopped.
- A pinch of salt and black pepper

DIRECTIONS:

1. In a pan that fits your air fryer, mix all the ingredients and whisk really well.

2. Introduce the pan in the fryer and cook at 400°F for 20 minutes. Divide into bowls and serve cold

Nutrition: Calories: 173; Fat: 8g; Fiber: 2g; Carbs: 4g; Protein: 11g

2. Mozzarella and Tomato Salad

Preparation Time: 17 minutes Servings: 6

INGREDIENTS:

- 1 lb. tomatoes; sliced
- 1 cup mozzarella; shredded
- 1 tbsp. ginger; grated
- 1 tbsp. balsamic vinegar
- 1 tsp. sweet paprika
- 1 tsp. chili powder
- . tsp. coriander, ground

DIRECTIONS:

1. In a pan that fits your air fryer, mix all the ingredients except the mozzarella, toss, introduce the pan in the air fryer and cook at 360°F for 12 minutes
2. Divide into bowls and serve cold as an appetizer with the mozzarella sprinkled all over.

Nutrition: Calories: 185; Fat: 8g; Fiber: 2g; Carbs: 4g; Protein: 8g

3. Garlic Cheese Dip

Preparation Time: 15 minutes Servings: 10

INGREDIENTS:

- 1 lb. mozzarella; shredded
- 6 garlic cloves; minced
- 3 tbsp. olive oil
- 1 tbsp. thyme; chopped.
- 1 tsp. rosemary; chopped.
- A pinch of salt and black pepper

DIRECTIONS:

1. In a pan that fits your air fryer, mix all the ingredients, whisk really well, introduce in the air fryer and cook at 370°F for 10 minutes.
2. Divide into bowls and serve right away.

Nutrition: Calories: 184; Fat: 11g; Fiber: 3g; Carbs: 5g; Protein: 7g

4. Crab and Artichoke Dip

Preparation Time: 25 minutes Servings: 4

INGREDIENTS:

- 8 oz. cream cheese, soft
- 12 oz. jumbo crab meat
- 1 bunch green onions; minced
- 14 oz. canned artichoke hearts, drained and chopped.
- 1 cup coconut cream
- 1 . cups mozzarella; shredded
- 1 tbsp. lemon juice
- 1 tbsp. lemon juice
- A pinch of salt and black pepper

DIRECTIONS:

1. In a bowl, combine all the ingredients except half of the cheese and whisk them really well.
2. Transfer this to a pan that fits your air fryer, introduce in the machine and cook at 400°F for 15 minutes

3. Sprinkle the rest of the mozzarella on top and cook for 5 minutes more. Divide the mix into bowls and serve as a party dip

Nutrition: Calories: 240; Fat: 8g; Fiber: 2g; Carbs: 4g; Protein: 14g

5. Bacon Snack

Preparation Time: 15 minutes • Servings: 4

INGREDIENTS

- 1cup dark chocolate; melted
- 4bacon slices; halved
- Apinch of pink salt

DIRECTIONS

1. Dip each bacon slice in some chocolate, sprinkle pink salt over them.
2. Put them in your air fryer's basket and cook at 350°F for 10 minutes

NUTRITION: Calories: 151; Fat: 4g; Fiber: 2g; Carbs: 4g; Protein: 8g

6. Shrimp Snack

Preparation Time: 15 minutes • Servings: 4

INGREDIENTS

- 1lb. shrimp; peeled and deveined
- ¼ cup olive oil
- 3garlic cloves; minced
- ¼ tsp. cayenne pepper
- Juice of ½ lemon
- A pinch of salt and black pepper

DIRECTIONS

1. In a pan that fits your air fryer, mix all the ingredients, toss,
2. Introduce in the fryer and cook at 370°F for 10 minutes
3. Servings as a snack

NUTRITION: Calories: 242; Fat: 14g; Fiber: 2g; Carbs: 3g; Protein: 17g

7. Avocado Wraps

Preparation Time: 20 minutes • Servings: 4

INGREDIENTS

- 2avocados, peeled, pitted and cut into 12 wedges
- 1tbsp. ghee; melted
- 12bacon strips

DIRECTIONS

1. Wrap each avocado wedge in a bacon strip, brush them with the ghee.
2. Put them in your air fryer's basket and cook at 360°F for 15 minutes
3. Servings as an appetizer

NUTRITION: Calories: 161; Fat: 4g; Fiber: 2g; Carbs: 4g; Protein: 6g

8. Cheesy Meatballs

Preparation Time: 30 minutes • Servings: 16 meatballs

INGREDIENTS

- 1lb. 80/20 ground beef.

- 3oz. low-moisture, whole-milk mozzarella, cubed

- 1large egg.

- ½ cup low-carb, no-sugar-added pasta sauce.

- ¼ cup grated Parmesan cheese.

- ¼ cup blanched finely ground almond flour.

- ¼ tsp. onion powder.

- tsp. dried parsley.

- ½ tsp. garlic powder.

DIRECTIONS

1. Take a large bowl, add ground beef, almond flour, parsley, garlic powder, onion powder and egg. Fold ingredients together until fully combined

2. Form the mixture into 2-inch balls and use your thumb or a spoon to create an indent in the center of each meatball. Place a cube of cheese in the center and form the ball around it.

3. Place the meatballs into the air fryer, working in batches if

necessary. Adjust the temperature to 350 Degrees F and set the timer for 15 minutes

4. Meatballs will be slightly crispy on the outside and fully cooked when at least 180 Degrees F internally.

5. When they are finished cooking, toss the meatballs in the sauce and sprinkle with grated Parmesan for serving.

NUTRITION: Calories: 447; Protein: 29.6g; Fiber: 1.8g; Fat: 29.7g; Carbs: 5.4g

9. Tuna Appetizer

Preparation Time: 15 minutes • Servings: 2

INGREDIENTS

- 1lb. tuna, skinless; boneless and cubed
- 3scallion stalks; minced
- 1chili pepper; minced
- 2tomatoes; cubed
- 1tbsp. coconut aminos
- 2tbsp. olive oil
- 1tbsp. coconut cream
- 1tsp. sesame seeds

DIRECTIONS

1. In a pan that fits your air fryer, mix all the ingredients except the sesame seeds, toss, introduce in the fryer and cook at 360°F for 10 minutes

2. Divide into bowls and serve as an appetizer with sesame seeds sprinkled on top.

NUTRITION: Calories: 231; Fat: 18g; Fiber: 3g; Carbs: 4g; Protein: 18g

10. Pickled Snack

Preparation Time: 25 minutes • Servings: 4

INGREDIENTS

- 4dill pickle spears; sliced in half and quartered
- 1cup avocado mayonnaise
- 8bacon slices; halved

DIRECTIONS:

1. Wrap each pickle spear in a bacon slice, put them in your air fryer's basket and cook at 400°F for 20 minutes.
2. Serve as a snack with the mayonnaise

NUTRITION: Calories: 100; Fat: 4g; Fiber: 2g; Carbs: 3g; Protein: 4g

11. Avocado Bites

Preparation Time: 13 minutes Servings: 4

INGREDIENTS

- 4avocados, peeled, pitted and cut into wedges
- 1½ cups almond meal
- 1egg; whisked
- A pinch of salt and black pepper
- Cooking spray

DIRECTIONS

1. Put the egg in a bowl and the almond meal in another.
2. Season avocado wedges with salt and pepper, coat them in egg and then in meal almond

3. Arrange the avocado bites in your air fryer's basket, grease them with cooking spray and cook at 400°F for 8 minutes Servings as a snack right away

NUTRITION: Calories: 200; Fat: 12g; Fiber: 3g; Carbs: 5g; Protein: 16g

12. Asparagus Wraps

Preparation Time: 20 minutes • Servings: 8

INGREDIENTS

- 16asparagus spears; trimmed
- 16bacon strips
- 1tbsp. lemon juice
- 2tbsp. olive oil
- 1tsp. oregano; chopped.
- 1tsp. thyme; chopped.
- A pinch of salt and black pepper

DIRECTIONS

1. Take a bowl and mix the oil with lemon juice, the herbs, salt and pepper and whisk well.
2. Brush the asparagus spears with this mix and wrap each in a bacon strip

3. Arrange the asparagus wraps in your air fryer's basket and cook at 390°F for 15 minutes.

NUTRITION: Calories: 173; Fat: 4g; Fiber: 2g; Carbs: 3g; Protein: 6g

13. Warm Tomato Salsa

Preparation Time: 13 minutes • Servings: 4

INGREDIENTS

- 2spring onions; chopped.
- 1garlic clove; minced
- 4tomatoes; cubed
- 3chili peppers; minced
- 2tbsp. lime juice
- 2tsp. parsley; chopped.
- 2tsp. cilantro; chopped.
- Cooking spray

DIRECTIONS

1. Grease a pan that fits your air fryer with the cooking spray and mix all the ingredients inside.

2 Introduce the pan in the machine and cook at 360°F for 8 minutes. Divide into bowls and serve

NUTRITION: Calories: 148; Fat: 1g; Fiber: 2g; Carbs: 3g; Protein: 5g

14. Zucchini Chips

Preparation Time: 20 minutes • Servings: 6

INGREDIENTS

- 3zucchinis, thinly sliced
- 1cup almond flour
- 2eggs; whisked
- Salt and black pepper to taste.

DIRECTIONS

1. Take a bowl and mix the eggs with salt and pepper. Put the flour in a second bowl.
2. Dredge the zucchinis in flour and then in eggs
3. Arrange the chips in your air fryer's basket, cook at 350°F for 15 minutes and serve as a snack.

NUTRITION: Calories: 120; Fat: 4g; Fiber: 2g; Carbs: 3g; Protein: 5g

CHAPTER 2

DESSERTS

15. Butter Cookies

Preparation Time: 30 minutes Servings: 12

INGREDIENTS:

- 2 eggs, whisked
- 2 . cup almond flour
- . cup swerve
- . cup butter; melted
- 1 tbsp. heavy cream
- 2 tsp. vanilla extract
- Cooking spray

DIRECTIONS:

1. Take a bowl and mix all the ingredients except the cooking spray and stir well.

2. Shape 12 balls out of this mix, put them on a baking sheet that fits the air fryer greased with cooking spray and flatten them

3. Put the baking sheet in the air fryer and cook at 350°F for 20 minutes

4. Serve the cookies cold.

NUTRITION: Calories: 234; Fat: 13g; Fiber: 2g; Carbs: 4g; Protein: 7g

16. Ginger Cookies

Preparation Time: 25 minutes Servings: 12

INGREDIENTS:

- . cup butter; melted
- 2 cups almond flour
- 1 cup swerve
- 1 egg
- . tsp. nutmeg, ground
- . tsp. cinnamon powder
- 2 tsp. ginger, grated
- 1 tsp. vanilla extract

DIRECTIONS:

1. Take a bowl and mix all the ingredients and whisk well.
2. Spoon small balls out of this mix on a lined baking sheet that fits the air fryer lined with parchment paper and flatten them
3. Put the sheet in the fryer and cook at 360°F for 15 minutes

4. Cool the cookies down and serve.

NUTRITION: Calories: 220; Fat: 13g; Fiber: 2g; Carbs: 4g; Protein: 3g

17. Chocolate Pudding

Preparation Time: 30 minutes Servings: 6

INGREDIENTS:

- 24 oz. cream cheese, soft
- 12 oz. dark chocolate; melted
- . cup heavy cream
- . cup erythritol
- 3 eggs, whisked
- 1 tbsp. vanilla extract
- 2 tbsp. almond meal

DIRECTIONS:

1. In a bowl mix all the ingredients and whisk well.
2. Divide this into 6 ramekins, put them in your air fryer and cook at 320°F for 20 minutes.

3.   Keep in the fridge for 1 hour before serving

Nutrition: Calories: 200; Fat: 7g; Fiber: 2g; Carbs: 4g; Protein: 6g

18. Cream Cheese Brownies

Preparation Time: 35 minutes Servings: 6

INGREDIENTS:

- 3 eggs, whisked
- . cup almond flour
- . cup coconut flour
- . cup almond milk
- 2 tbsp. cocoa powder
- 3 tbsp. swerve
- 6 tbsp. cream cheese, soft
- 3 tbsp. coconut oil; melted
- 1 tsp. vanilla extract
- . tsp. baking soda
- Cooking spray

DIRECTIONS:

1. Grease a cake pan that fits the air fryer with the cooking spray.
2. Take a bowl and mix rest of the ingredients, whisk well and pour into the pan

3. Put the pan in your air fryer, cook at 370°F for 25 minutes, cool the brownies down, slice and serve.

Nutrition: Calories: 182; Fat: 12g; Fiber: 2g; Carbs: 4g; Protein: 6g

19. Coconut and Avocado Cake

Preparation Time: 45 minutes Servings: 6

INGREDIENTS:

- 1 cup coconut, shredded

- 1 cup mashed avocado

- 2 tbsp. ghee; melted

- 3 tbsp. stevia

- 1 tsp. cinnamon powder

- 2 tsp. cinnamon powder

DIRECTIONS:

1. Take a bowl and mix all the ingredients and stir well.

2. Pour this into a cake pan lined with parchment paper, place the pan in the fryer and cook at 340°F for 40 minutes.

Cool the cake down, slice and serve

Nutrition: Calories: 192; Fat: 4g; Fiber: 2g; Carbs: 5g; Protein: 7g

20. Creamy Chia Seeds Pudding

Preparation Time: 35 minutes Servings: 6

INGREDIENTS:

- 2 cups coconut cream
- . cup chia seeds
- 6 egg yolks, whisked
- 1 tbsp. ghee; melted
- 2 tbsp. stevia
- 2 tsp. cinnamon powder

DIRECTIONS:

1. Take a bowl and mix all the ingredients, whisk, divide into 6 ramekins, place them all in your air fryer and cook at 340°F for 25 minutes. Cool the puddings down and serve

Nutrition: Calories: 180; Fat: 4g; Fiber: 2 carbs 5g; Protein: 7g

21. Awesome Chinese Doughnuts

Preparation Time: 10 minutes • Cooking Time: 8 minutes • Servings: 8

INGREDIENTS

- 1tbsp. baking powder
- 6tbsps. coconut oil
- ¾ cup of coconut milk
- 2tsps. sugar
- 2cup all-purpose flour
- ½ tsp. sea salt

DIRECTIONS

1. Preheat the air fryer to 3500F.
2. Mix baking powder, flour, sugar, and salt in a bowl.
3. Add coconut oil and mix well. Add coconut milk and mix until well combined.
4. Knead dough for 3-4 minutes.
5. Roll dough half inch thick and using cookie cutter cut doughnuts.

6. Place doughnuts in cake pan and brush with oil. Place cake pan in air fryer basket and air fry doughnuts for 5 minutes. Turn doughnuts to other side and air fry for 3 minutes more.

7. Serve and enjoy.

NUTRITION: Calories: 259 Fat: 15.9 g Carbs: 27 g Protein: 3.8 g

22. Crispy Bananas

Preparation Time: 10 minutes • Cooking Time: 10 minutes • Servings: 4

INGREDIENTS

- 4sliced ripe bananas
- 1egg
- ½ cup breadcrumbs
- 1½ tbsps. cinnamon sugar
- 1tbsp. almond meal
- 1½ tbsps. coconut oil
- 1tbsp. crushed cashew
- ¼ cup corn flour

DIRECTIONS

1. Set the pan on fire to heat the coconut oil over medium heat and add breadcrumbs in the pan and stir for 3-4 minutes.
2. Remove pan from heat and transfer breadcrumbs in a bowl.
3. Add almond meal and crush cashew in breadcrumbs and mix well.

4. Dip banana half in corn flour then in egg and finally coat with breadcrumbs.

5. Place coated banana in air fryer basket. Sprinkle with Cinnamon Sugar.

6. Air fry at 350 F/ 176 C for 10 minutes.

7. Serve and enjoy.

NUTRITION: Calories: 282 Fat: 9 g Carbs: 46 g Protein: 5 g

23. Air-Fried Banana and Walnuts Muffins

Preparation Time: 10 minutes Cooking Time: 10 minutes

Servings: 2

INGREDIENTS

- ¼ cup flour
- ½ tsp. baking powder
- ¼ cup mashed banana
- ¼ cup butter
- 1tbsp. chopped walnuts
- ¼ cup oats

DIRECTIONS

1. Spray four muffin molds with cooking spray and set aside.
2. In a bowl, mix together mashed bananas, walnuts, sugar, and butter.
3. In another bowl, mix oat flour, and baking powder.
4. Combine the flour mixture to the banana mixture.
5. Pour batter into prepared muffin mold.

6. Place in air fryer basket and cook at 320 F/ 160 C for 10 minutes.

7. Remove muffins from air fryer and allow to cool completely.

8. Serve and enjoy.

NUTRITION: Calories: 192 Fat: 12.3 g Carbs: 19.4 g Protein: 1.9 g

24. Air-Fryer Blueberry Muffins

Preparation Time: 10 minutes • Cooking Time: 14 minutes • Servings: 2

INGREDIENTS

- 1/3 cup milk
- 2tbsps. sugar
- 2/3 cup flour
- ¾ cup blueberries
- 3tbsps. melted butter
- 1egg
- 1tsp. baking powder

DIRECTIONS

1. Spray four silicone muffin cups with cooking spray and set aside.
2. In a bowl, mix together all ingredients until well combined.
3. Pour batter into prepared muffin cups.
4. Place muffin cups in air fryer basket and cook at 320 F/ 160 C for 14 minutes.

5. Serve and enjoy.

NUTRITION: Calories: 435 Fat: 20.9 g Carbs: 55 g Protein: 9 g

25. Nutty Mix

Preparation Time: 5 minutes • Cooking Time: 4 minutes •
Servings: 6

NUTRITION:

- Calories: 316
- Fat: 29 g
- Carbs: 11.3 g
- Protein: 7.6 g
- Ingredients:
- 2cup mix nuts
- 1tsp. ground cumin
- 1tsp. chili powder
- 1tbsp. melted butter
- 1tsp. salt
- 1tsp. pepper

DIRECTIONS

1. Set all ingredients in a large bowl and toss until well coated.
2. Preheat the air fryer at 3500F for 5 minutes.

3. Add mix nuts in air fryer basket and air fry for 4 minutes. Shake basket halfway through.

4. Serve and enjoy.

26. Vanilla Spiced Soufflé

Preparation Time: 20 minutes • Cooking Time: 32 minutes • Servings: 6

INGREDIENTS

- ¼ cup all-purpose flour
- 1cup whole milk
- 2tsps. vanilla extract
- 1tsp. cream of tartar
- 1vanilla bean
- 4egg yolks
- 1-oz. sugar
- ¼ cup softened butter
- ¼ cup sugar
- 5egg whites

DIRECTIONS

1. Combine flour and butter in a bowl until the mixture becomes a smooth paste.
2. Set the pan over medium flame to heat the milk. Add sugar and stir until dissolved.

3. Mix in the vanilla bean and bring to a boil.

4. Beat the mixture using a wire whisk as you add the butter and flour mixture.

5. Lower the heat to simmer until thick. Discard the vanilla bean. Turn off the heat.

6. Place them on an ice bath and allow to cool for 10 minutes.

7. Grease 6 ramekins with butter. Sprinkle each with a bit of sugar.

8. Beat the egg yolks in a bowl. Add the vanilla extract and milk mixture. Mix until combined.

9. Whisk together the tartar cream, egg whites, and sugar until it forms medium stiff peaks.

10. Gradually fold egg whites into the soufflé base. Transfer the mixture to the ramekins.

11. Put 3 ramekins in the cooking basket at a time. Cook for 16 minutes at 330 degrees. Move to a wire rack for cooling and cook the rest.

12. Sprinkle powdered sugar on top and drizzle with chocolate sauce before serving.

NUTRITION: Calories: 215 Fat: 12.2g   Carbs: 18.98g Protein: 6.66g

27. Apricot Blackberry Crumble

Preparation Time: 10 minutes • Cooking Time: 20 minutes • Servings: 8

INGREDIENTS

- 1cup flour
- 18oz. fresh apricots
- 5tbsps. cold butter
- ½ cup sugar
- 5½ oz. fresh blackberries
- Salt
- 2tbsps. lemon juice

DIRECTIONS

1. Put the apricots and blackberries in a bowl. Add lemon juice and 2 tbsps. of sugar. Mix until combined.
2. Transfer the mixture to a baking dish.
3. Put flour, the rest of the sugar, and a pinch of salt in a bowl. Mix well. Add a tbsp. of cold butter.
4. Combine the mixture until it becomes crumbly. Put this on top of the fruit mixture and press it down lightly.

5. Set the baking tray in the cooking basket.

6. Cook for 20 minutes at 390 degrees.

7. Allow to cool before slicing and serving.

NUTRITION: Calories: 217 Fat: 7.44g   Carbs: 36.2g
Protein: 2.3g

28. Chocolate Cup cakes

Preparation Time: 5 minutes • Cooking Time: 12 minutes • Servings: 6

INGREDIENTS

- 3eggs
- ¼ cup caster sugar
- ¼ cup cocoa powder
- 1tsp. baking powder
- 1cup milk
- ¼ tsp. vanilla essence
- 2cup all-purpose flour
- 4tbsps. butter

DIRECTIONS

1. Preheat your Air Fryer to a temperature of 400°F (200°C).
2. Beat eggs with sugar in a bowl until creamy.
3. Add butter and beat again for 1-2 minutes.
4. Now add flour, cocoa powder, milk, baking powder, and vanilla essence, mix with a spatula.
5. Fill ¾ of muffin tins with the mixture and place them

into Air Fryer basket.

6. Let cook for 12 minutes.

7. Serve!

NUTRITION: Calories: 289 Protein: 8.72 g Fat: 11.5 g Carbs: 38.94 g

29. Stuffed Baked Apples

Preparation Time: 3 minutes • Cooking Time: 12 minutes • Servings: 4

INGREDIENTS

- 4tbsps. honey
- ¼ cup brown sugar
- ½ cup raisins
- ½ cup crushed walnuts
- 4large apples

DIRECTIONS:

1. Preheat Air Fryer to a temperature of 350°F (180°C).
2. Cut the apples from the stem and remove the inner using spoon.
3. Now fill each apple with raisins, walnuts, honey, and brown sugar.
4. Transfer apples in a pan and place in Air Fryer basket, cook for 12 minutes.
5. Serve.

NUTRITION: Calories: 324 Protein: 2.8 g Fat: 6.99 g Carbs: 70.31 g

30. Roasted Pineapples with Vanilla Zest

Preparation Time: 5 minutes • Cooking Time: 8 minutes • Servings: 4

INGREDIENTS

- 2anise stars
- ¼ cup orange juice
- 1tsp. lime juice
- 1vanilla pod
- 2tbsps. caster sugar
- ¼ cup pineapple juice
- 1lb. pineapple slices

DIRECTIONS

1. Preheat Air Fryer to a temperature of 350°F (180°C).
2. Take a baking pan that can fit into Air Fryer basket.
3. Now add pineapple juice, sugar, orange juice, anise stars, and vanilla pod into a pan and mix well.
4. Place in pineapple slices evenly and transfer pan into Air Fryer basket.

5. Cook for 8 minutes.

6. Serve!

NUTRITION: Calories: 90   Protein: 0.79 g Fat: 1.17 g Carbs: 23.22 g

31. Vanilla Coconut Pie

Preparation Time: 15 minutes • Cooking Time: 12 minutes • Servings: 4

INGREDIENTS

- Shredded coconut, 1 cup
- Granulated monk fruit, ½ cup
- Vanilla extract, 1 ½ tsps.
- Eggs,
- Almond milk, 1 ½ cup
- Coconut flour, ½ cup
- Butter, ¼ cup

DIRECTIONS

1. Combine all the ingredients in a suitable mixing bowl using a wooden spatula to form a batter.
2. Pour this batter into a 6-inch pie pan then place this pan in the air fryer basket.
3. Return the basket to the air fryer then cook the pie for 12 minutes at 3700 F on Air Fry Mode.

4. Allow it to cool then serve.

NUTRITION: Calories: 272   Fat: 27 g   Carbs: 7.8 g   Protein: 5.3 g

32. Veggie Quesadilla

Preparation Time: 15 minutes • Servings: 2

INGREDIENTS

- 4flatbread dough tortillas
- ⅔ cup shredded pepper jack cheese
- ½ medium avocado; peeled, pitted and mashed
- ½ medium green bell pepper; seeded and chopped
- ¼ cup diced red onion
- ¼ cup chopped white mushrooms
- ¼ cup full-fat sour cream.
- ¼ cup mild salsa
- 1tbsp. coconut oil

DIRECTIONS

1. In a medium skillet over medium heat, warm coconut oil. Add pepper, onion and mushrooms to skillet and sauté until peppers begin to soften, 3–5 minutes

2. Place two tortillas on a work surface and sprinkle each with half of cheese. Top with sautéed veggies, sprinkle

with remaining cheese and place remaining two tortillas on top

3. Place quesadillas carefully into the air fryer basket.

4. Adjust the temperature to 400 Degrees F and set the timer for 5 minutes.

5. Flip the quesadillas halfway through the cooking time. Serve warm with avocado, sour cream and salsa.

943. **NUTRITION:** Calories: 795; Protein: 34.5g; Fiber: 6.5g; Fat: 61.3g; Carbs: 19.4g

33. Cajun Olives and Peppers

Preparation Time: 16 minutes • Servings: 4

INGREDIENTS

- ½ lb. mixed bell peppers; sliced
- 1cup black olives, pitted and halved
- ½ tbsp. Cajun seasoning
- 1tbsp. olive oil

DIRECTIONS:

1. In a pan that fits the air fryer, combine all the ingredients.
2. Put the pan it in your air fryer and cook at 390°F for 12 minutes. Divide the mix between plates and serve

NUTRITION: Calories: 151; Fat: 3g; Fiber: 2g; Carbs: 4g; Protein: 5g

34. Chili Broccoli

Preparation Time: 20 minutes • Servings: 4

INGREDIENTS:

- 1lb. broccoli florets
- Juice of 1 lime
- 2tbsp. chili sauce
- 2tbsp. olive oil
- A pinch of salt and black pepper

DIRECTIONS

1. Take a bowl and mix the broccoli with the other ingredients and toss well.
2. Put the broccoli in your air fryer's basket and cook at 400°F for 15 minutes
3. Divide between plates and serve.

NUTRITION: Calories: 173; Fat: 6g; Fiber: 2g; Carbs: 6g; Protein: 8g

35. Balsamic Kale

Preparation Time: 14 minutes • Servings: 6

INGREDIENTS

- 2½ lb. kale leaves
- 3garlic cloves; minced
- 2tbsp. olive oil
- 2tbsp. balsamic vinegar
- Salt and black pepper to taste.

DIRECTIONS

1. In a pan that fits the air fryer, combine all the ingredients and toss.
2. Put the pan in your air fryer and cook at 300°F for 12 minutes. Divide between plates and serve

NUTRITION: Calories: 122; Fat: 4g; Fiber: 3g; Carbs: 4g; Protein: 5g

36. Mustard Greens and Green Beans

Preparation Time: 22 minutes • Servings: 4

INGREDIENTS

- 1lb. green beans; halved

-

- ¼ cup tomato puree
- 3garlic cloves; minced
- 1bunch mustard greens, trimmed
- 2tbsp. olive oil
- 1tbsp. balsamic vinegar
- Salt and black pepper to taste.

DIRECTIONS

1. In a pan that fits your air fryer, mix the mustard greens with the rest of the ingredients, toss, put the pan in the fryer and cook at 350°F for 12 minutes

2. Divide everything between plates and serve.

NUTRITION: Calories: 163; Fat: 4g; Fiber: 3g; Carbs: 4g; Protein: 7g

37. Olives and Cilantro Vinaigrette

Preparation Time: 17 minutes • Servings: 4

INGREDIENTS

- 1cup baby spinach
- 2cups black olives, pitted
- 1tbsp. olive oil
- 2tbsp. balsamic vinegar
- A bunch of cilantro; chopped.
- Salt and black pepper to taste.

DIRECTIONS

1. In a pan that fits the air fryer, combine all the ingredients and toss.
2. Put the pan in the air fryer and cook at 370°F for 12 minutes

3. Transfer to bowls and serve.

NUTRITION: Calories: 132; Fat: 4g; Fiber: 2g; Carbs: 4g;
Protein: 4g

38. Broccoli and Tomatoes

Preparation Time: 20 minutes • Servings: 4

INGREDIENTS

- 1broccoli head, florets separated
- 2cups cherry tomatoes, quartered
- 1tbsp. cilantro; chopped.
- Juice of 1 lime
- A drizzle of olive oil
- A pinch of salt and black pepper

DIRECTIONS

1. In a pan that fits the air fryer, combine the broccoli with tomatoes and the rest of the ingredients except the cilantro, toss, put the pan in the air fryer and cook at 380°F for 15 minutes

2   Divide between plates and serve with cilantro sprinkled on top.

NUTRITION: Calories: 141; Fat: 3g; Fiber: 2g; Carbs: 4g; Protein: 5g

39. Kale and Mushrooms

Preparation Time: 20 minutes • Servings: 4

INGREDIENTS

- 1lb. brown mushrooms; sliced
- 1lb. kale, torn
- 14oz. coconut milk
- 2tbsp. olive oil
- Salt and black pepper to taste.

DIRECTIONS

1. In a pan that fits your air fryer, mix the kale with the rest of the ingredients and toss
2. Put the pan in the fryer, cook at 380°F for 15 minutes, divide between plates and serve

NUTRITION: Calories: 162; Fat: 4g; Fiber: 1g; Carbs: 3g; Protein: 5g

40. Spicy Olives and Avocado

Preparation Time: 20 minutes • Servings: 4

INGREDIENTS

- 2small avocados, pitted; peeled and sliced
- ¼ cup cherry tomatoes; halved
- 2cups kalamata olives, pitted
- 1tbsp. coconut oil; melted
- juice of 1 lime

DIRECTIONS:

1. In a pan that fits the air fryer, combine the olives with the other ingredients, toss.
2. Put the pan in your air fryer and cook at 370°F for 15 minutes

3. Divide the mix between plates and serve.

NUTRITION: Calories: 153; Fat: 3g; Fiber: 3g; Carbs: 4g; Protein: 6g

41. Lemon Endives

Preparation Time: 20 minutes • Servings: 4

INGREDIENTS

- 12endives, trimmed
- 3tbsp. ghee; melted
- 1tbsp. lemon juice
- A pinch of salt and black pepper

DIRECTIONS

1. take a bowl and mix the endives with the ghee, salt, pepper and lemon juice and toss.
2. put the endives in the fryer's basket and cook at 350°f for 15 minutes
3. divide between plates and serve.

NUTRITION: Calories: 163; Fat: 4g; Fiber: 3g; Carbs: 5g; Protein: 6g

42. Roasted Lemon Cauliflower

Preparation Time: 20 minutes • Servings: 4

INGREDIENTS

- 1medium head cauliflower
- 1medium lemon.
- 2tbsp. salted butter; melted.
- 1tsp. dried parsley.
- ½ tsp. garlic powder.

DIRECTIONS

1. Remove the leaves from the head of cauliflower and brush it with melted butter. Cut the lemon in half and zest one half onto the cauliflower. Squeeze the juice of the zested lemon half and pour it over the cauliflower.
2. Sprinkle with garlic powder and parsley. Place cauliflower head into the air fryer basket. Adjust the temperature to 350 Degrees F and set the timer for 15 minutes
3. Check cauliflower every 5 minutes to avoid overcooking. It should be fork tender.

4. To serve, squeeze juice from other lemon half over cauliflower. Serve immediately.

NUTRITION: Calories: 91; Protein: 3.0g; Fiber: 3.2g; Fat: 5.7g; Carbs: 8.4g

43. Strawberry Fudge Brownies

Preparation time: 15 minutes Cooking time: 20 minutes Servings: 16

INGREDIENTS

- ½ cup melted butter 2/3 cup swerve
- ½ tsp vanilla extract
- room temperature eggs
- ½ cup almond flour
- 1/3 cup unsweetened cocoa powder 1 Tbsp plain, unsweetened gelatin
- ½ tsp salt
- ½ tsp baking powder
- ¼ cup water
- ½ cup fresh chopped strawberries

DIRECTIONS

1 Preheat your air fryer to 325 degrees F and grease an 8x8 inch square baking pan.

2 Combine the melted butter, vanilla extract, swerve, and melted butter in a bowl and whisk together well.

3 Add the cocoa powder, almond flour, baking powder, gelatin, and salt and whisk again until smooth.

4   Add the water and stir again. Fold in the strawberries

5   Pour the batter into the greased baking pan and place in the preheated air fryer. Bake for 15 minutes. The center will seem a little wet while the edges will be more firm- this is perfect.

6   Let the brownies cool in the pan before slicing and serving.

NUTRITION: Calories 193, Total Fat 10g, Saturated Fat 4g, Total Carbs 11g, Net Carbs 6g, Protein 3g, Sugar 5g, Fiber 5g, Sodium 283mg, Potassium 412g

44. Cheesecake Fudge Brownies

Preparation time: 15 minutes Cooking time: 20 minutes Servings: 16

INGREDIENTS

- ½ cup cream cheese, softened 3 Tbsp erythritol sweetener
- ½ cup melted butter 2/3 cup swerve
- ½ tsp vanilla extract
- room temperature eggs
- ½ cup almond flour
- 1/3 cup unsweetened cocoa powder 1 Tbsp plain, unsweetened gelatin
- ½ tsp salt
- ½ tsp baking powder
- ¼ cup water

DIRECTIONS

1. Preheat your air fryer to 325 degrees F and grease an 8x8 inch square baking pan.
2. In a small bowl, mic the cream cheese and erythritol sweetener together. Set aside.

3. Combine the melted butter, vanilla extract, swerve, and melted butter in a bowl and whisk together well.

4. Add the cocoa powder, almond flour, baking powder, gelatin, and salt and whisk again until smooth.

5. Add the water and stir again.

6. Pour the batter into the greased baking pan and swirl in the cream cheese mix.

7. Place the pan in the preheated air fryer. Bake for 15 minutes. The center will seem a little wet while the edges will be more firm- this is perfect.

8. Let the brownies cool in the pan before slicing and serving.

NUTRITION: Calories 215, Total Fat 18g, Saturated Fat 5g, Total Carbs 6g, Net Carbs 3g, Protein 3g, Sugar 2g, Fiber 3g, Sodium 283mg, Potassium 316g

45. Chocolate Chip Cookies

Preparation time: 10 minutes Cooking time: 9 minutes Servings: 12

INGREDIENTS

- ½ cup butter, melted
- ¾ cup erythritol
- 1 tsp vanilla extract 1 egg
- 1 ½ cups almond flour
- ½ tsp salt
- ½ tsp baking powder
- ¾ cup sugar free chocolate chips

DIRECTIONS

1. Preheat your air fryer to 330 degrees F and prepare your air fryer tray with a piece of parchment.
2. Beat the melted butter and erythritol together in a large bowl.
3. Add the eggs and vanilla and mix until the batter comes together.
4. Add the salt, baking powder and almond flour and mix until a nice, smooth batter forms.
5. Fold in the chocolate chips then scoop the cookie dough onto the prepared sheet tray. You will want to leave about 2 inches

between the cookie dough scoops as the dough will spread slightly. If needed, you can bake the cookies in batches.

6. Bake the cookies in the air fryer for 8-9 minutes or until golden brown on the edges.

7. Let cool on the sheet tray for 5 minutes before removing and enjoying!

NUTRITION: Calories 168, Total Fat 18g, Saturated Fat 6g, Total Carbs 2g, Net Carbs 1g, Protein 4g, Sugar 1g, Fiber 1g, Sodium 342mg, Potassium 110g

46. Butter Cookies

Preparation time: 10 minutes Cooking time: 9 minutes Servings: 12

INGREDIENTS

- ½ cup butter, melted
- ¾ cup erythritol
- 1 tsp vanilla extract 1 egg
- 1 ½ cups almond flour
- ¼ tsp xanthan gum
- ½ tsp salt
- ½ tsp baking powder

DIRECTIONS

1. Preheat your air fryer to 330 degrees F and prepare your air fryer tray with a piece of parchment.
2. Beat the melted butter and erythritol

   together in a large bowl.
3. Add the eggs and vanilla and mix until the batter comes together.

4. Add the salt, baking powder, xanthan gum and almond flour and mix until a nice, smooth batter forms.

5. Scoop the cookie dough onto the prepared sheet tray. You will want to leave about 2

6. inches between the cookie dough scoops as the dough will spread slightly. If needed, you can bake the cookies in batches.

7. Bake the cookies in the air fryer for 8-9 minutes or until golden brown on the edges.

8. Let cool on the sheet tray for 5 minutes before removing and enjoying!

NUTRITION: Calories 110, Total Fat 12g, Saturated Fat 3g, Total Carbs 1g, Net Carbs 0g, Protein 3g, Sugar 0g, Fiber 1g, Sodium 342mg, Potassium 46mg

47. Walnut Cookies

Preparation time: 10 minutes Cooking time: 9 minutes Servings: 12

INGREDIENTS

- ½ cup butter, melted
- ¾ cup erythritol
- 1 tsp vanilla extract 1 egg
- 1 ½ cups almond flour
- ½ tsp salt
- ½ tsp baking powder
- ¾ cup chopped walnuts

DIRECTIONS

1. Preheat your air fryer to 330 degrees F and prepare your air fryer tray with a piece of parchment.
2. Beat the melted butter and erythritol together in a large bowl.
3. Add the eggs and vanilla and mix until the batter comes together.
4. Add the salt, baking powder and almond flour and mix until a nice, smooth batter forms.

5. Fold in the walnuts then scoop the cookie dough onto the prepared sheet tray. You will want to leave about 2 inches between the cookie dough scoops as the dough will spread slightly. If needed, you can bake the cookies in batches.

6. Bake the cookies in the air fryer for 8-9 minutes or until golden brown on the edges.

7. Let cool on the sheet tray for 5 minutes before removing and enjoying!

NUTRITION: Calories 174, Total Fat 18g, Saturated Fat 6g, Total Carbs 2g, Net Carbs 1g, Protein 7g, Sugar 1g, Fiber 1g, Sodium 342mg, Potassium 178g

48. Coconut Cookies

Preparation time: 10 minutes Cooking time: 9 minutes Servings: 12

INGREDIENTS

- ½ cup butter, melted
- ¾ cup erythritol
- 1 tsp vanilla extract 1 egg
- 1 cup almond flour
- ½ cup coconut flour
- ½ tsp salt
- ½ tsp baking powder
- ½ cup unsweetened coconut flakes

DIRECTIONS

1. Preheat your air fryer to 330 degrees F and prepare your air fryer tray with a piece of parchment.
2. Beat the melted butter and erythritol together in a large bowl.
3. Add the eggs and vanilla and mix until the batter comes together.

4. Add the salt, baking powder coconut flour and almond flour and mix until a nice, smooth batter forms.

5. Fold in the coconut flakes then scoop the cookie dough onto the prepared sheet tray. You will want to leave about 2 inches between the cookie dough scoops as the dough will spread slightly. If needed, you can bake the cookies in batches.

6. Bake the cookies in the air fryer for 8-9 minutes or until golden brown on the edges.

7. Let cool on the sheet tray for 5 minutes before removing and enjoying!

NUTRITION: Calories 178, Total Fat 16g, Saturated Fat 7g, Total Carbs 7g, Net Carbs 4g, Protein 5g, Sugar 3g, Fiber 3g, Sodium 342mg, Potassium 278g

49. Almond Cookies

Preparation time: 10 minutes Cooking time: 9 minutes Servings: 12

INGREDIENTS

- ½ cup butter, melted
- ¾ cup erythritol
- 1 tsp almond extract 1 egg
- 1 ½ cups almond flour
- ½ tsp salt
- ½ tsp baking powder
- ¾ cup chopped almonds

DIRECTIONS

1. Preheat your air fryer to 330 degrees F and prepare your air fryer tray with a piece of parchment.
2. Beat the melted butter and erythritol together in a large bowl.
3. Add the eggs and almond extract and mix until the batter comes together.
4. Add the salt, baking powder and almond flour and mix until a nice, smooth batter forms.

5. Fold in the chopped almonds then scoop the cookie dough onto the prepared sheet tray. You will want to leave about 2 inches between the cookie dough scoops as the dough will spread slightly. If needed, you can bake the cookies in batches.

6. Bake the cookies in the air fryer for 8-9 minutes or until golden brown on the edges.

7. Let cool on the sheet tray for 5 minutes before removing and enjoying!

NUTRITION: Calories 176, Total Fat 24g, Saturated Fat 6g, Total Carbs 4g, Net Carbs 1g, Protein 6g, Sugar 1g, Fiber 3g, Sodium 348mg, Potassium 311g

50. Chocolate Chip Almond Cookies

Preparation time: 10 minutes Cooking time: 9 minutes Servings: 12

INGREDIENTS

- ½ cup butter, melted
- ¾ cup erythritol
- 1 tsp almond extract 1 egg
- 1 ½ cups almond flour
- ½ tsp salt
- ½ tsp baking powder
- ½ cup sugar free chocolate chips
- ¼ cup sliced almonds

DIRECTIONS

1. Preheat your air fryer to 330 degrees F and prepare your air fryer tray with a piece of parchment.
2. Beat the melted butter and erythritol together in a large bowl.
3. Add the eggs and almond extract and mix until the batter comes together.
4. Add the salt, baking powder and almond flour and mix

until a nice, smooth batter forms.

5. Fold in the sliced almonds then scoop the cookie dough onto the prepared sheet tray. You will want to leave about 2 inches between the cookie dough scoops as the dough will spread slightly. If needed, you can bake the cookies in batches.

6. Bake the cookies in the air fryer for 8-9 minutes or until golden brown on the edges.

7. Let cool on the sheet tray for 5 minutes before removing and enjoying!

NUTRITION: Calories 174, Total Fat 19g, Saturated Fat 7g, Total Carbs 3g, Net Carbs 1g, Protein 5g, Sugar 1g, Fiber 2g, Sodium 342mg, Potassium 281g

CONCLUSION

I hope this book was able to help you to understand the benefits of an Air Fryer and the basics on how to use it. The next step is to plan your meals and gather the ingredients. This appliance is easy to use and you will eventually get the hang of the process. Once you have tried several recipes, you can already start tweaking the ingredients to create variations or start making your own.

Enjoy the process of preparing your meals in a healthier way using this innovation when it comes to cooking.

CPSIA information can be obtained
at www.ICGtesting.com
Printed in the USA
BVHW061406250321
603170BV00020B/900